Samuel Bampfylde Windsor

Three Sermons on the Parable of the Prodigal Son

Preached in the Cathedral Church of St. George, Kingston, Canada West

Samuel Bampfylde Windsor

Three Sermons on the Parable of the Prodigal Son
Preached in the Cathedral Church of St. George, Kingston, Canada West

ISBN/EAN: 9783744762175

Printed in Europe, USA, Canada, Australia, Japan

Cover: Foto ©Lupo / pixelio.de

More available books at **www.hansebooks.com**

THREE SERMONS

ON THE

𝔓arable of the 𝔓rodigal 𝔖on.

PREACHED IN THE

𝔈athedral 𝔈hurch of 𝔖t. 𝔊eorge,

KINGSTON, CANADA WEST.

BY

SAMUEL B. WINDSOR, M.A.,

CHAPLAIN TO THE FORCES.

·

Price, Twenty-Five Cents.

KINGSTON :

CREIGHTON, PRINTER.

1867.

ADVERTISEMENT.

It is not because I think the following Sermons especially worthy of general notice that I publish them. I am thoroughly aware of their many defects, and how far they fall short even of my own ideal.

But some of the Congregation who heard them expressed a wish to have them, and an opinion that their publication would do good. In deference to their judgment I print them, with an earnest hope that they may, by God's blessing, be profitable either for warning or encouragement, as may be needed.

S. B. W.

Kingston, C. W.,
 Whitsuntide.

SERMON I.

The first steps in evil.

Many of you, my brethren, if you have not turned to
them in your Bibles, will wonder where these words occur :
others who remember them, who have just looked for them,
or to whom I now state that they are in the parable of the
Prodigal Son, will, I dare say, think that I have done
strangely in separating them thus from their context, if
they do not in their secret hearts esteem it a mere garb-
ling of a text.   Before then we enter upon their consideration, let me tell you my reasons, and then I trust such
impressions will be removed.

The Bible is not like any other book.   There is indeed
a school existing now which maintains that it is, and that
it is to be criticised and interpreted exactly like every
other book.   God forbid, my brethren, that any of us
should ever adopt an opinion so disparaging to its honor,
so irreverently forgetful that it is the Book of Books, the
word of God.   There are many other books which, as far
as mere history goes, are to most people quite as interest-
ing, quite as engrossing, quite as beautifully written as it
is ; but there is one essential difference.   When once you
have mastered them in all the depth of their meaning, you
may indeed, for your own gratification, read them again
and again ; and as often as you repeat your perusal, so
often are you delighted with the repetition of the same
charms which so pleased you at first.   But in the case of
the Bible, no thoughtful, reverent student of it can have
failed to remark that the more it is read the more meaning you find in it.   The very words which you thought
you knew and understood, will have in them a new and
deeper significance ; and this not one or twice, but con-
tinually, so that you are forced to confess that it is inex-

haustible. You can fathom the productions of mere human intellect. What God has had written for our learning is like a rich mine; it gives up new treasures the deeper and the oftener we dig into it. This seems to me to be one of the meanings—only one mark you—of that declaration of Christ our Lord when He said "the words which I speak unto you, they are spirit and they are life." There is just that difference between Holy Scripture and any other writings that there is between the Living Face and the most exquisite portrait. Be this last never so beautiful, it can but render one expression. But there is literally no end to the phases of the other. And while we freely admit there is much to admire, much to delight, much to thank God for in the productions of human genius, there is a deadness and sameness in them which they cannot escape from, and which is to be found everywhere save in the evernew, everliving oracles of the everlasting God.

And if this be true, my brethren, and I dare venture to affirm that very few will deny it, how must it apply especially to those parts of it which record the words of the blessed Jesus? Do you not see how very irreverent it is to suppose for one moment that He ever used words at random, or that there is not a propriety, aye! and a deep significance too, if we could only understand it, in every form of expression that He used? He who created speech used it, not to conceal His thoughts, still less to dilute their force by needless ornament, but as an engine to convey living truth..

To apply this to the passage before us.—The grand scope of the parable is, no doubt, to depict the wonderful mercy and love of God the Father towards repentant sinners; but besides this there are two other very important doctrines set forth. The one, the sure and rapid fall into the worst sin, of those who once begin to cast off restraint. The other, that though the state of the forgiven penitent is blessed indeed, the blessedness of him who has never fallen is greater still by far.

It would be impossible to do justice to all these three subjects in one sermon. I propose this evening to confine myself to that which I conceive is the first taught in the parable. I mean the rapid deterioration of every one after he has deliberately overleaped the first barrier.

There are two ways of understanding the first portion of the parable, and estimating the character of the prodigal. Most persons look on him only as one who has left the ways of godliness and plunged headlong into sin and dissipation. This, I incline to think, is a mistake. It overlooks the graphic portraiture of his gradual though rapid declension, and so it loses all the lessons to be drawn from the wonderful analogy which subsists between it and the spiritual life of alas! too many of us.

I would rather interpret his character less severely.— It seems that his case was this—a young man entering into life with the new tastes, desires and impulses of early manhood strong within him. He thinks himself old enough to enjoy them, and cannot understand, and is disinclined to tolerate the petty and vexatious restraints which living under his father's roof he has to bear. His first request, then, is not, I think, an expression of intention to do what afterwards indeed he did, viz: depart altogether from his father's neighbourhood and reach ; it was only the desire, not an uncommon one methinks, to be and to feel himself independent of control.

His father had probably watched his character for some time. It may have been with the distinct object of making him buy his experience, or it may have been that as the lad was legally of age he had no power to keep him at home. Any how the request is granted ; and "*not many days after*" he gathers all his possessions and goes far away, where no remonstrance can reach him, and where the continual sight of his father's well ordered house, and his elder brother's good conduct, may be no more an eyesore and a reproach.

How, when in that far country, he wasted his substance in riotous living; how he grew to learn the utter vanity and unsatisfying nature of such things; how in the desperation of actual want and hunger, he submitted to the deepest degradation; and how, after all, he found it of no use, the parable goes on to tell. We may perhaps presently recur to them and draw out their spiritual analogies. At present I revert to my text. You will see now why I chose the words, and will admit that they are the words in the whole parable to express the fact to which I want to call your serious attention. It is this: when once we deliberately cast off the wise and loving restraints which a Father, be he our earthly or our heavenly Father, places around us, it is the beginning of the end: it is then only a question of time how soon, in the expressive language of the present day, we go to the bad altogether. But it is very soon, "*not many days after,*" that we seek for greater freedom—more complete emancipation from restraint.

What is the ordinary course of young men when once they enter upon life? I am not speaking of those who "stay at home with God," who make Him the guide of their youth, in sure and certain hope that He will be the support of their age. That, alas that we should say so, that is the *extra*ordinary course. It is the exception, not the rule. Is not one of the very first marks of a lad's having become his own master, the doing something, no matter what, which he was forbidden to do before? It may be a thing in itself harmless, and only withheld from motives of prudence, or until he is old enough. But do not young men as a rule try to assert themselves? Do they not think it manly to break rules, just for the sake of breaking them? Woe to those who do, for unless quick repentance follow, the next step will be to remove themselves as quickly as they can out of the reach of any one who can, any one who is likely to speak a word of advice, or make an attempt to control them. But while I mention this to shew you how true a picture of human life, even in this, one of its secondary objects, the parable presents, I am rather concerned to shew its truthfulness in the spiritual life. And it makes no manner of difference what you take to have been the primary meaning of the parable, concerning which there have been many most diverse opinions, some supposing the elder son to mean the angels, and the younger man; some interpreting this last to mean the Gentiles, and the other the Jews; others, and this is the explanation which seems best, because most universally practical, understanding simply by the two sons the two great classes into which, as all Scripture testifies, mankind is divided, viz: those who serve and worship God, and those who serve Him not. We, however, may limit this meaning still further, and consider the case of the one whom we are considering as that of one who has fallen from the worship of God.

It is to one who has fallen from grace that that which is the main scope of the parable, God's infinite love and ready forgiveness of penitents is so inexpressibly comforting. It is such a one alone whom the portion of it which we are considering contemplates. But how true a picture it presents to our gaze! Under this aspect we see a man, not necessarily young in years, only immature in true wisdom, beginning to cast away the wholesome restraints of religion. He does not see, for instance, why he should go to Church so regularly as he has been, from his boyhood upwards, taught to do. Not that he means to neglect to worship God; but cannot he do so at home, and in private as well? He begins to think the strict observance of the Lord's day very necessary perhaps for the many, the uneducated, but he has grown beyond that. He looks on daily morning and evening prayer, and reading God's word as very right, proper indeed to be insisted on for children and young people, but as trammels on the free spiritual worship wherewith a mature man should approach God.

Such, or such like, are the delusions by which men who have no idea at the time of wilfully setting God and His commandments at nought, who only feel chafed and irritated at what they call these formal restrictions, deceive their own souls and pave the way for their utter abandonment of all godliness. If you tell them what will be the issue, they very earnestly disclaim any such intention, nor do they mean it: but when once they have taken the first step, when once they have broken through the wholesome restraints which early religious training has placed upon them, "not many days after" they too gather all their substance together and go into a far country. It is different with them and with those who have never had the blessings of a religious education. If they had never known better things it might not have been so; but the very fact that they have been religiously brought up makes their own inconsistency so apparent, renders the reproaches of their conscience so keen, that they plunge into deeper sin, they go further from God in order to prevent their feeling them. For the far country is a state of sin. Man, it is true, cannot remove himself actually from God, but he can depart from Him in heart; and he who has once begun to try to escape from the ordinary and appointed ways of acknowledging Him, will not be long before he tries to exclude Him from his very memory.

Now in this, as in that which the parable sets forth in its words, there is the same cause at bottom, viz: impatience of control, a restless desire to be under no restriction. Young men in this world have to learn by bitter experience that to be under authority is a very happy state, and that to kick against the pricks is only a mark of their want of wisdom; and in like manner the perfect submission of the will of God, the recognizing Him in small things as well as great, the ready bowing to His authority, the zealous observance of all that tends to shew Him honor and respect, as it is the mark of true wisdom, so those who fail in it have taken the first steps in the ways of ungodliness, and will soon be on the high road that leadeth to destruction. Virtually they are already companions of the fool who saith in his heart "there is no God" and very soon the Psalmist's sequel will be true of them too, "corrupt are they, and become abominable in their wickedness; there is none that doeth good, no not one."

In the parable, as soon as the young man has got quit of his father's dictation and advice, he follows the natural bent of his sinful desires, and wastes his health, strength and substance in dissipation and excess. Regardless of the future, forgetful of the past, he lives in the present as long as his means last; and then, in distress and want, is obliged perforce to submit himself to far more rigorous control than that from which he had been so anxious to escape, and reduced to perform menial offices of a nature that his very soul abhors, to avoid perishing from starvation. Only then does he begin to recognise the error of his ways, and to wish he had acted more wisely; and how expressive are the words that it was "when he came to himself," that he resolved on retracing his steps.

In our spiritual life, of which this is a picture, we see exactly the same course. As soon as a man has once begun openly to disregard God and His laws, then there is no limit to the ungodliness to which he gives himself up. All his best gifts, his reason, his eloquence, his every talent, he prostitutes to the service of sin. But when he has done his utmost and his worst, when there is nothing more that he can do, what has he gained? he is sated, yet dissatisfied; and there comes on him that mighty famine, that craving of the soul which God alone, and nothing earthly, nothing devilish can fill.

Do you not believe, my brethren, that there is many a

one sold into sin, running greedily after inquity, who in his heart of hearts, when he feels, as he cannot but feel, the utter emptiness of this world and its pleasures, do not you believe that he in his lucid intervals, when he comes to himself—for sin is madness, and nothing else—longs for the days that are gone, wishes that the past could be un-done, and bitterly regrets his first departure from the ways af God, his impatient rebellion and violation of His wise and loving restraints? Though he may not acknowledge it, even to himself, in words, how, when he is weary and heavy laden, must he long for the "easy yoke and light burthen" of the Master whom so short a time back he de-serted !

Did you ever know of the death-bed confessions of any great sinner which did not bear testimony that all his sin-fulness began by the violation of some of the simpler forms and practices of religion, whence the descent was so quick, easy and rapid that he could not trace his down-ward course. Believe me, my brethren, they were no mere words of course, that it was not to round a period, or for a rhetorical ornament, but because they embody a deep and most important truth that our blessed Lord in-troduced into His parable these words of my text. The very heathen knew and recognized this truth. Easy is the descent towards hell, said one of old, but to return, to retrace one's steps heavenward, that is indeed a work of difficulty. We know that it is more than that : we know that it would be, and is, an utter impossibility but for the love and mercy of Him whom the heathen knew not, but whom we adore.

But it does not fall in with the subject that I have pro-posed to myself this evening, to touch on the hope that is set before us, so beautifully shewn in the middle portion of the parable. My desire is to impress on the minds of all, young and old, how fearfully dangerous it is, not to take the first steps in sin, that most will admit, but to pull down or overleap the barriers which act as safeguards between us, and any overt act. And yet how common is this fault. How few there are who are contented to remain in a state of dependence ; how wide-spread the destructive notion that we can stand alone. Secret irritation at the exercise of any authority over him, and a real alienation in heart from his Father, went before the prodigal son's request. For it has been well noticed that there is a studied use of legal terms in the original, as if to shew that if there were any refusal he was prepared to stand upon his rights. And no one begins to neglect the outward worship of God, to set at naught His day, to be negligent in prayer, whose heart has not long before been far from Him. " The apostacy of the heart will often precede the apostacy of the life." For a long time his secret will is totally at variance with God's will, albeit the divergence is not seen because he keeps up the outer semblance of respect ; but this cannot be very long. Except in a few, it is to be hoped, rare cases, such hypocrisy is too irksome to be maintained. At last he boldly lays claim to freedom from all these restrictions—meaning very often to go no further—but that has become impossible ; the stone once set rolling cannot be stopped. Having taken the first step, the next is infinitely easier—and it is *not many days* before the downward course is begun, and he far on his way thither.

It sometimes, indeed, does happen by God's great mercy that all the bitter fruit which wilful sin bears, is not in every case shewn forth. Some miracle of mercy arrests the sinner on his course ; but the teaching of the parable is plain, that the worst conceivable wickedness, the most utter profligacy, is only the legitimate and natural result of the first wilful departure from God. And I have been striving to shew you that it also teaches us that this first overt act is, in most cases, prefaced by a long nourished, and at last, expressed discontent of rules and restrictions.

And before I conclude let me point out to you another application of this great truth no less important at the present time. We have fallen upon days which seem to be heralding the advent of Anti-Christ. Not only, as I said at first, is the Bible to be interpreted as any other book, but there are those who deny its genuineness and authenticity, who impeach its veracity, and repudiate its inspiration; and together with these we find, as natural allies, a school which would ignore or set aside the Creeds, set little store on distinctive doctrines, and so far from contending for the faith once delivered to the Saints, maintain that it remains for this nineteenth century to discover and elaborate the true faith. Yet these persons are, apparently many of them, men of piety and most holy life; and all declare with one voice the most thorough allegiance to, and love of our Lord and Saviour Jesus Christ.

But apply all that we have been saying here, and is it not manifest that from some reason or other, they are in the condition of the prodigal son. They want to be released from all restraints, and when they have effected their desire, can we doubt where they will be led; far from God, far from Christ, with whose avowed or masked deniers they have already associated themselves; far from every thing which is good and holy, into the barren and cold region of heartless scepticism. May God grant, my brethren, that none of us, nor any whom we love, may go so fearfully astray.

And now with one or two words I will conclude. You observe that the Father in the parable grants at once his son's request. You know that in our own experience there is no force exercised by God to keep us in the right way, nor to hinder our following the devices of our own hearts; and does not this thought bring to our minds, with great force, the words of the Apostle Peter, which at once describe what we are, and what we should not be: "As free and not using our liberty as a cloke of maliciousness, but as the servants of God." Brethren, there is no paradox here, no contradiction, we are free, but we are servants too ; we are free to choose our service, but a master we must have; we must either put up with the tyrannical rule and harsh despotism, and most cruel bondage of sin and him who is the prince of sin, or we may be, if we will, servants of Him Whose service is perfect freedom. His own master man never was, never can be ; and if he kick against the restraints, and sullenly disobey the rules which a merciful God and Father prescribes to keep us in the right way, he is doing more than he thinks or means ; he is giving place to the devil, and preparing himself for a total alienation from God—for open and debasing profligacy or avowed scepticism. Is it not then our wisdom, should it not be our chief aim, our daily prayer, to render to God the willing homage of ready obedience and loving hearts, content to be checked in our wayward fancies, to be restrained in our wanton and unchastened longing, knowing that "He does not willingly grieve nor afflict the children of men," and that the annoyances and vexations which we meet with, the crossings of our wills which we have to put up with, are not only good for discipline, but actual proofs of His love ?

My brethren, let these thoughts, these principles, actuate us all. May those who are young be contented to suffer restraints, and willingly obey their parents and those who are set over them ; for contempt and disregard of an earthly father is virtually contempt and disregard of God, and will inevitably lead to it. May we shun and pray against the temptations which would lead us to disparage the Apostles' doctrine and fellowship, the Creeds and other safeguards of the faith. Finally, may we all give diligent heed to guard against that passive rebellion of the will which always goes before disobedience, and which shews itself in reluctant acknowledgment and grudging homage of Him from Whom come all our blessings, in Whom consists our strength, without Whom we must perish and come to a fearful end.

May these thoughts stir us up to a more thorough acknowledgment of God in all the details of our daily life, to a more willing, more hearty service, that so if we have commenced to wander we may at once return ; if we have been inclined to assert our independence we may trample the temptation under foot, and staying at home with God may hear, day by day, as we progress in the Christian life, and look to Him, our Father, for help and strength and grace, may hear, I say, those blessed words, " Son thou art ever with me—all that I have is thine."

SERMON II.

Forgiveness.

When five weeks ago, I preached to you on the first portion of the parable from which I have also taken this text just read to you, I endeavoured to justify the selection of words which I then made by shewing that there was contained in them the essence, so to speak, of the lesson to be learned; which was, as many of you will recollect, the exceeding danger of rebelling against the wholesome restraints of lawful authority, because of the rapid declension into the worst forms of evil after the first step once taken.

My subject this evening is what I then told you is the second great doctrine of the parable. I mean God's full, free, entire forgiveness of the sinner upon his repentance. And though there are very many passages in the scriptures alike of the Old and New Testament which declare this gracious truth, and though there are many other texts which might appropriately stand at the commencement of a sermon treating of it, yet I do not think that there is any to be found in the whole length and breadth of the Bible, from Genesis to Revelations, so suitable as the one which I have chosen; because, as I shall hope to shew you, none which tells so clearly, yet in such few words the largeness of God's grace.

There was a practical experience of God's forgiveness in the case of our first parents, in that they did not at once reap the full reward of their transgression; and from that time up to the giving of the law from Mount Sinai, there was abundant evidence of God's long suffering and forbearance, whence men might, and no doubt did, infer the reality of this comfortable truth. But the first declaration of it was when the Lord Almighty was pleased to reveal himself to Moses, and to proclaim His name. Then, for the first time, we find it set down in explicit terms as the attribute of God that He is one "keeping mercy for thousands, forgiving iniquity and transgression," though there was immediately added, " and that will by no means clear the guilty." And then followed many a long year, in which this was felt and realized, so that the Psalmist was able in one place (Ps. ciii.) to speak of God in words of thankful praise as one " who forgiveth all thy sins, and healeth all thine iniquities," and in another (Ps. cxxx.), having a just view, that it was God's omnipotence and eternity which was especially manifested in this attribute, " There is forgiveness with thee that thou mayest be feared :" and it was in the full appreciation of this that the prophet Micah exclaims (vii. 18), " Who is a God like unto thee, that pardoneth iniquity, and passeth by the transgression of the remnant of His heritage ? He retaineth not His anger forever, because He delighteth in mercy."

But as it pleased God to reveal to His prophets the future glory of the Redeemer's Kingdom, their perception of, and declarations on this subject, grew clearer and more frequent. Jeremiah the Prophet, referring to the return from captivity, which was in some measure a type of Israel's future restoration, has these glorious words : " I will cleanse them from all their iniquity whereby they have sinned against me, and I will pardon all their iniquities whereby they have sinned and whereby they have transgressed against me." But when he was given to declare the New Covenant the promises which he then uttered on this subject were better still, viz. : " I will forgive their iniquities, and I will remember their sins no more"—words quoted, as you may all remember, twice by the Great Apostle of the Gentiles, because in them is so evidently shadowed forth the washing away of man's sin in the Redeemer's blood. But though in these

passages, and many more of like import might be added,
and from the New Testament many stronger still—though,
I say, in those passages, God's forgiveness is explicitly
and fully declared—there yet lacks something which
would enable a sinner beginning to be conscious of his
transgressions to appropriate them personally, and to
apply them to his own individual case.

It is this which the parable supplies :—and the words of
it which I have chosen go further ; for they not only declare God's forgiveness of the individual sinner, but in a
most affecting way set forth the gracious truth that He,
as it were, meets him half way, that He gives every encouragement to his repentance, that He responds to the
secret wishes of the heart.

My brethren, an abstract truth may be the foundation
of much that is practical, but it has no attraction for the
mass of men, except they can be shewn that they have a
personal interest in it. And the great truth that God does
forgive sinners is a thing no doubt for which to be deeply
grateful, and to adore God's mercy ; but it will have little
or no effect in encouraging men to repent and betake
themselves to God, except in the case of each individual
it be shewn that God is willing to forgive him ; then it
may have its effect. Now the teaching of this parable does
this :—It depicts not mankind as a body, falling into sin,
but it gives the portraiture of one individual, and that so
vividly, so graphically, that every one that hears it cannot but say in his heart, "It is I who am here described."
Therefore in the blessed sequel which describes the rich
mercy and abundant grace of God the Father towards the
repentant prodigal, it is still the same individual who is
pardoned. Each one, therefore, who has felt that the first
portion describes himself, may, if he fulfil the condition,
in like manner appropriate to himself the certainty of forgiveness. For this reason I say that the passage is pre-
eminently fit to stand at the head of a sermon of which

the object is to declare God's forgiveness and pardoning love.

But we meet with a certain amount of difficulty as we proceed to consider it, even on the very threshhold. It was easy to shew how true is the picture of man's sinful perverseness, which the former part of the parable sets forth. Many, if not all, practically know it. But is it all, is it many, is it more than a very very few who have an experimental knowledge of God's mercy following on their repentance? Some there are, I doubt not, who have; and they will readily bear testimony to its truth and blessedness. But the many have yet to learn it, and it is they whose attention to the teaching of this parable I earnestly request. What could have been more perverse, more wilful, than the prodigal's conduct? How many among ourselves would have been disposed to overlook or to forgive the like? Yet in the very first evidence of his penitence he is pardoned by his Father, and treated almost as though he had never transgressed. Surely there is no need of any laboured proof to convince you that the meaning of this is that so shall the case be with us, yea, with the worst sinner among us, so soon as God sees in us a genuine repentance. The words of Isaiah shall be fulfilled, "though your sins be as scarlet they shall be white as snow, though they be red like crimson they shall be as wool."

It is impossible to exaggerate the confident assurance of forgiveness which each one of us may gather from the consideration of this passage. It is, and may be, as it assuredly has been, a source of inexpressible comfort and hope to all who feel themselves to have sinned and done wickedly, and who are led by God's grace to meditate repentance. But remember that it is only on repentance that God will forgive, and this is most unmistakeably set forth here.

What is repentance? Not, as many mistakenly suppose, sorrow for sin. That is indeed, sooner or later, in all true repentance, an accompaniment of it. It is a change in the disposition of the heart, evidenced in a changed life. Did the prodigal manifest this? Look at the parable. His pain and suffering, unrelieved by the desperate remedies which in his recklessness he has tried, bring him at last to himself. In a moment of calm reflection he sees the folly of his course, and how far better it had been for him never to have acted as he had done : nay how much better it will still be to submit to all that he had rebelled against, so as to get quit of his present misery. And in this spirit he first sacrifices his pride, for he resolves, having thrown away his right to the privileges of a sin, to be content with the lowest place in his Father's household ; and having thus resolved, he makes no delay, but acts at once on his resolution, and retraces his steps. Undo what he has done he cannot, but he does all he can, he makes up his mind to leave the service of his present tyrant, to brave the ridicule of his present companions, in hunger and thirst and wretchedness to toil on his weary way back again, trusting that his Father whose love which though he has so outraged, he yet recognizes will listen to his penitent confession, and not refuse his prayer.

Is it possible to depict the beginning of a real repentance more graphically? Can spiritual things be more thoroughly, more vividly set before us by earthly ones?

This is the course, my brethren, which every one must pursue if they would obtain God's forgiveness. We too must retrace our steps, we must break the chains that hold us, we must be content to bear scoffing and ridicule, we must be ready, aye gratefully ready, to accept the lowest place in God's kingdom, we must be prepared to make unreserved confession of our sin and unworthiness, and we must put our resolves into action. This is all hard to resolve, harder still to do; but there is no hope for us without it, whereas if we will and do act thus, there will be forgiveness for us too, as there was for the prodigal.

This, however, is far from all the teaching which we may gather from this plan of Holy Scripture. There may be some, who in their inner hearts are conscious of greater sin, more complete desertion of God than most are guilty of; and such may think that though there is forgiveness for very gross sinfulness, yet is there none for theirs. Then let me explain what we learn from the consideration of one expression in the parable which is very often passed over or misunderstood.

When on occasion of the mighty famine the prodigal began to be in want, it is said he hired himself out to a citizen of that country, who sent him into his fields to feed swine. Till then we may conceive, that though he adopted the manners and customs of that far country, he yet recognized himself as being, and was held by them to be an alien. But in his distress he, as it were, sacrifices his real citizenship, as far as he can, and by accepting service becomes naturalized there.

What can this mean, brethren, in the interpretation which fits the spiritual life of us but this? A man may be a very gross and habitual sinner, and yet not willingly give up the idea that some day he means to repent, and that it will be all right at the last. A man may go very far, and yet not deny God, nor like Pharaoh ignore Him. But the consequence of continued habits of willful sin is, sooner or latter, a sense of a void that would but cannot be filled, an aching craving of the soul, to which the pangs of bodily hunger are nothing in comparison. How should it be otherwise? It was in the image of God that man was created, and we cannot obliterate it. As St. Augustine says: "Thou madest us for Thyself, and our heart is restless till it repose on Thee." Well! my brethren, if the grace of God does not at this period of the sinner's career lead him to repent, what is his course? Is it not that he trys to drown the voice of conscience and dull the stings of remorse by still more desperate wickedness ? It is the remembrance of what he was that causes his agony. He will disown his former self. It is a fear of God which causeth his anguish. He will deny Him, and go over wholly to His enemy. Surely, my brethren, it is this which is here pictured ; that extremity of wickedness, "even in the lowest depth a deeper still," to which despair, and the agonized strivings to quiet the miserable unrest from which he is suffering, lead the sinner. And it is because this, the extremest condition of the sinner, is here portrayed, and because even to such a one pardon is vouchsafed, that I deem this whole parable so unspeakably comforting, and so full of value. Consider this well, and no one need fear that he has sinned past God's power and will to pardon.

But I would have you notice that though the prodigal had thus sinned, though he had thus outraged and set at nought his Father, though, as I have been explaining, he had done his worst to alienate himself from him, yet he does not, cannot forget that the relation does exist. Though he acknowledges, and is prepared to confess, yea though he does confess that he is unworthy to be called a son, and though he craves for a place in the household, rather of a menial servant than of a son—yet it is as his Father that he approaches him, it is by that name that he calls him. Can we doubt it is because he feels the impossibility of utterly severing that tie, that he has the courage to seek, that he gains the confidence to hope for pardon ? Now what does this teach us, my brethren ? Surely it is expressed in the words of the Psalmist, " Like as a father pitieth his children, so the Lord pitieth them that fear Him." It was the especial and distinctive promise of the New Covenant that God would be a Father to those who were admitted into it in a different and superior way from that in which the Jews regarded Him as such. And there is nothing which the Apostles more insist upon in their teaching. Witness St. Paul to the

Romans, viii.: "Ye have not received the spirit of bondage again to fear, but the spirit of adoption, whereby we cry Abba Father." And to the Galatians (iv. 4-7): "God sent forth His Son . . . . . that we might receive the adoption of sons; and because ye are sons God hath sent forth the Spirit of His Son into your hearts, crying Abba Father." And St. John: "Beloved *now* are we the sons of God." And it is in reference to this, which had then come to pass, that the Apostle St. Paul (2 Cor. vi.), admonishing the Corinthians of their sins, reminds them of the covenant, " Come out from among them, and be ye separate, and I will receive you, and will be a Father unto you, and ye shall be my sons and daughters, saith the Lord Almighty."

These words, these declarations, apply to us.

Now if it aggravates sin, as it most surely does, that it has been committed against One who is not only our Ruler and our God, but who has been pleased to constitute Himself our Father, and to receive us as His children, yet is it in the fact of this blessed relationship that our best hope of pardon consists. We, too, like the prodigal, have gone very far astray. We have kicked at the restraints of God's providence. We have broken His commandments. We have done our utmost to escape from Him. Nay, some of us may have denied Him, and gone over deliberately to the service of His enemy. Be it so. Yet do we learn here that if we will only resolve to repent— if we will make up our mind to forsake our sins, and do our first works—if we will come to Him as our Father, confessing our vileness, but yet claming our adoption, even while we admit our unworthiness, and pleading the merits of that true and only begotten Son by and through whom we have obtained this grace of sonship, God will shew Himself a Father to us. He will meet us half way. He will blot out, as a thick cloud, our transgressions, and as a cloud our sins. Only let us return unto him, and

He will forgive our inqiuity, and remember our sins no more. But it is, and must be, because we are sons, and for and through the merits of His dearly beloved Son Jesus Christ.

And it seems if it were for the especial encouragement of us Christians who have fallen into sin, and who, therefore, might justly fear lest this aggravation of it shut us out from God's pardon, that our blessed Lord delivered this parable of a disobedient, and rebellious, and subsequently pardoned *son*. And so there are few passages in all Holy Scripture which have been so effective in setting forth God's love, and in awakening repentance as this which is now before us.

But there are one or two other points to notice. I do not insist on that which my text sets forth, and which not one of you can fail to observe—how God's readiness to pardon is beautifully shewn in the Father seeing the prodigal a great way off, (doubtless, He was longing for his return, and had often wistfully looked out for him), and then running to meet him, and greeting him so lovingly, so forgivingly. What is of still more importance to observe is, that this did not hinder the confession which he had resolved to make. Now this is not merely a proof of the reality of the portraiture, an evidence of the master hand which delineated the character. It embodies a very important doctrine. It teaches us that though God's pardon is certain, aye pledged—yet we must seek it—seek it in humility of spirit—seek it with confession of our unworthiness. There are many that cannot understand this. There are many that reason thus with themselves—"God knows all things—He knows that I am repentant—what need of saying it in words?" I will not say if the prodigal had not confessed he would not have been forgiven; his very return was evidence of repentance and humility, but with ourselves God requires the actual confession, just as He requires prayer, albeit every one knows that He knoweth all things, and therefore all our necessities before we can utter them. This (in the matter of confession of sin) is very plainly set forth in the 32nd Psalm, which I quote from the Prayer Book version as probably most familiar : " Blessed is he whose unrighteousness is forgiven : and whose sin is covered. Blessed is the man unto whom the Lord imputeth no sin : and in whose spirit there is no guile. For while I held my tongue my bones consumed away through my daily complainings. For Thy hand is heavy upon me day and night: and my moisture is like the drought in summer. I will acknowledge my sin unto thee : and my unrighteousness have I not hid. I said, I will confess my sins unto the Lord : and so thou forgavest the wickedness of my sin." There is forgiveness with God my brethren. It is His most god-like attribute, the very proof of His omnipotency. But it is only for us, upon a deep conviction of sin, evidenced in a real repentance and hearty confession.

There are many other points in the parable full of beauty and expressiveness, from every one of which we might gather instruction, but time fails ; yet one other consideration must not be omitted. It is not set forth in the parable that anything except his suffering, moved the prodigal to repentance. But if you think of the other two short parables with which the chapter opens, and which, being in their general teaching identical with it, may not without violence be severed from it,—I mean the parables of the lost sheep, and lost piece of money, in which the shepherd and the woman are represented as using all dili- gence to recover the lost one of their possessions,—I say if you think of this you cannot but perceive that in the spiritual application of the parable we are reminded of our Blessed Lord's own words that He came " To *seek* and to save those that were lost." The Father in the parable did not seek his son. God *does* seek *us*. His invisible agen- cies are ever at work, ministering to our salvation, in the way most conducive to it, if only we do not resist their operations. It is often by pain and suffering and by experiencing the discomforts of sin that we too are first led to the thought of forsaking it; and so St. Paul says, "Godly sorrow worketh repentance not to be repented of," which is more correctly and forcibly translated the "pain, which is according to God's will, worketh a repentance which will cause no remorse, and whose issue is salvation."

If the Father in the parable could have controlled and influenced the circumstances of his son, would he not have ordered them exactly as they happened. My brethren, God can and does overrule not only the whole course of this world, but all the events that influence each individual, be he the most insignificant among us. Yea, the very hairs of our heads are numbered. It is not chance but God's will that causes us when we have transgressed some one of His commandments to suffer the consequences of it. Men talk of the natural consequences of this or that. They mean the results which, by God's laws impressed on the material as well as spiritual world always follow certain actions. Why He has so ordered the universe we cannot wholly know. One reason is revealed to us. He has made pain and suffering of one sort or another to follow every infraction of His rules, in order to induce us to forsake our sins, to bring us on our knees before Him, to persuade us to come within the sphere of His pardoning love. God waiteth to be gracious. He willeth not the death of a sinner. He is not willing that any should perish, but that all should come to repentance. But when he says, "I have no pleasure in the death of him that dieth, He adds, "Wherefore turn ye and live." He is ready to receive us, willing to pardon. His grace is about and around us for us to receive if only we accept His mercy and His love. But it rests with ourselves.

Only if we are willing, if in our hearts we be prepared

to forsake all, and follow Christ, though we have only taken one or two steps on the right way, He our ever loving, ever watchful Father, who readeth the heart, who needeth not that any should testify to Him of men, because He knoweth what is in man, He seeth us when we are a great way off, and will go forth by His Holy Spirit to meet us, and will pardon us without reproach, and will make us glad with the joy of His salvation. "And there shall be joy in Heaven and before the Angels of God over one sinner that repenteth more than over ninety and nine just persons who need no repentance."

SERMON III.

The Reward of Obedience.

NOTE.—This Sermon was preached in place of one which had been announced by the Bishop of the Diocese on Obedience.

LUKE xv. 31—*Son thou art ever with me, and all that I have is thine.*

These words, my brethren, as doubtless every one here recollects, are a part, and that the most important part, of the answer which the Father of the Prodigal Son made in reply to the reproaches which the elder brother addressed to him, because of what he thought was overweening joy and merriment on occasion of that prodigal's return. They will form, with God's blessing, the subject of our meditations this evening. I told you, when on two previous occasions I discoursed from this parable, that there was a third lesson besides those which I dwelt upon to be deduced from it. That lesson, I conceive, is contained in the words of my text, when rightly understood ; and it is one not wholly alien from that which was announced to be the subject this evening of him whose place I now occupy. Before, however, we enter on their full consideration, I must ask your attention while I endeavour to correct one or two erroneous notions which I think too generally prevail respecting this portion of the parable. Most people are so absorbed in the consideration of God's love to sinners, as set forth in the father's forgiveness of his prodigal son, and are disposed so to magnify it, (not unduly indeed, for how can it be made too much of? but) so exclusively to think of it, that they lose sight of other equally important teaching ; seize only on the words of the elder brother, which their very contrast to the father's spirit brings into prominence ; set him down at once as jealous and unforgiving ; build on this an explanation, which they seem to consider the chief, if not the only one, that the elder brother signifies the Jews and the younger the Gentiles, or this one the Publicans and

sinners, and that the Pharisees, and then exalt the repentant one far above the one who needed no repentance, if
they do not end by esteeming this last an uninteresting,
despicable character.

This is one mistake, arising partly from what I have
have said, partly from not observing the wonderful praise
and commendation contained in the words of the text,
and the marvellous privileges declared to be his to whom
such praise is due.

And another error which is in some measure built up
on this former one, is that terribly false doctrine, that
very snare of the evil one, which underlies the proverb,
common I dare say to every one of you, but them which
I venture to assert none is more ungodly, none more un-
true—"the greater the sinner the greater the saint." I
say it is built on the former error. They see the prodigal
forgiven, and think of the blessedness of his state; they
do not observe the greater blessedness of the other, and
they do magnify one feature in the story which they in-
correctly set down as a trait, a distinctive trait in his
character, and condemn him for it. As a consequence,
in their reading of the parable, the repentant sinner is
more blessed than the never fallen saint. I desire to pro-
test against this error, at the same time that I endeavour
to enlarge upon the true view of the elder brother's
character. But some one will say, Is there not Scripture
warrant for this interpretation which you condemn? Do
not the very words of the chapter, twice repeated, bear
testimony to its truth; " There is joy in Heaven over one
sinner that repenteth more than over ninety and nine just
men that need no repentance." No, my brethren, it is
not so. Consider a moment. Is joy upon an unexpected
arrival a mark of love beyond that which is bestowed on
others? Surely not. Take the cases of the two short
parables which come before this one in the chapter. Do
you value a piece of money that has been found after

its loss, more than one which you never lost? It is
absurd to think it. Joy is a manifestation of turbulent
delight; it is more noisy, but not so deep, not so lasting
as happiness, and has not necessarily any connection with
love. The joy in the case of the two parables, is because
of the unexpectedness of the gratification. The excessive,
as the elder son thought, manifestation of welcome to the
returning prodigal, was no proof of excessive love. It
was but the natural mark of the happiness which this
unexpected recovery of him, as it were from the dead,
could not but call forth. And so the father explains it:
"It was meet that we should make merry and be glad,
for this thy brother was dead and is alive again, he was
lost and is found." I believe that incalculable mischief
has arisen from the misunderstanding this point. You
can all bear me witness, who heard my last sermon on the
subject, that I am in no wise disposed to diminish the
largeness of God's forgiving love as here set forth: I then
said, and I again repeat, that there are no limits to His
pardon, no bounds to His grace, but such as a man himself sets, by neglecting to believe in His offers of mercy,
by forgetting that He is our Father, by not pleading the
merits of His dear Son. But, as I told you then, there is
a blessedness higher still; and that is theirs who have
never strayed from God, who have never disobeyed Him:
for to such God says, as in the words of the text, "All
that I have is thine."

But let me endeavour to explain the difficulty which I
know so many feel, and which, till I learned better, I felt
too; the seeming jealousy of the elder brother. Does it
not arise from misunderstanding the mode of teaching by
parable? There are Divine truths to be taught, and in
Christ's mercy and wisdom He couches them in a tale of
this earth. It is sufficient if the great lessons are therein
contained, and we must not suppose that every little inci-
dental trait which makes the picture more life-like and at-

tractive is of equal importance with its grander features. Now in this parable there were two phases of human life to be depicted; one that of the sinner who had gone wilfully astray, had become penitent and was forgiven; the other, the far more uncommon one of the man, who from his youth up had served God with an honest and true heart, and who therefore needed no such forgiveness. But they are in each case human beings, who are the types of the two classes, and the best of such is far from perfect. The feeling of jealousy, therefore, which the elder brother manifests is not to be understood as his distinctive characteristic, it is only as I said of another part of the parable, on a previous occasion, one of those slight touches which show the Master Hand of Him who delineated the character. He *is* represented as well nigh perfect; as much so as mere man could be. He were more than man if he were faultless. And remember, it is after we have suffered that we learn sympathy, after we have erred and received pardon that we grow willing to forgive. This experience he lacked. And that he did fail in this matter, we may almost be thankful; for if it had not been so, neither he or we should have heard, at least on that occasion, the gracious words of the text. And there is yet one word more to add before we proceed to the consideration of them. It is this, to bid you observe that after these words were addressed to him by his father all remonstrance ceased. The sense of his own higher privileges, and more blessed state, must at once have dispelled his gloom, made him also willing to welcome the prodigal, and not grudge him his share of their common father's love. For though I know that the opposite view is more commonly held, I pray you to notice that Scripture is silent on the point, and the supposition that he still continued in his unloving disposition is mere assumption, and, I think, inconsistent with the character of one so highly blessed because so nearly perfect.

And now, my brethren, I invite you to the thoughtful consideration of his state, and its privileges as set forth in the words of the text. I said that my subject would not be altogether alien from that which was announced, and which you expected to hear treated. I mean obedience, and I think you will see I am borne out in what I said ; for what do these words describe but a condition of perfect obedience and its consequent reward. The departure of the prodigal first from his father's house, and afterwards from his very neighbourhood meaned, as I shewed you, a spirit of rebellion against restraint, followed up by overt acts of disobedience. And the consequent suffering and misery, shadowed forth the chastisements wherewith God corrects those who neglect or refuse to obey Him, and whereby He graciously endeavours to lead them to repentance. The conduct then of the eldest son, the course of whose whole life is summed up in these brief words of praise, is as evidently meant to shew the opposite ; that is, as I have said, perfect unswerving obedience. Nor need we be surprised that so much is said about the one; so little about the other. Not only is the younger son's character by far the commoner, and, therefore, the more needful to be exhibited in all its aspects for our contemplation, but also the brevity of the record of the eldest son's life is of itself a presumption of his superiority. It has passed into a proverb that the country is happy whose history is dull ; for that which breaks monotony is little else than a record of wars, disturbances and crimes in the annals of nations. And so it is with human life. And this parable is only a Divine example of and sanction to the truth that whereas it takes many words to write the tale of most men's lives, comprising as it must the narrative of, at its best, sharp contests with temptation, of unchastened longings hardly repressed, if not of grievous sins, frequent shortcomings, perhaps deep repentance, and then too often, continual backslidings, followed, it may be, by renewed penitence, it is possible to express in one line the even tenor of his way, who stays at home with God, and rests in Him.

I said on the last occasion of my preaching on this parable, that though many could appreciate the truthfulness of the description of the prodigal's career, comparatively few had experienced the blessings of forgiveness following repentance. But who *is* there who can out of his own consciousness describe the condition of the perfectly obedient ? Certainly not he who now addresses you. And who of his own personal knowledge and experience could say, if such a task were attempted that such description is true. I trow not one.

And yet, my brethren, there can be no doubt that these words, like every other portion of Holy Scripture, were written for our learning. And, therefore, we may hope that God's blessing will rest upon us if we do our best in endeavouring to gain even an approximate idea of that great blessedness. We may sometimes gain our best conceptions of things beyond our reach, by contemplating their contraries. Notice then what an illustration of our text, in this direction, may be found in the earliest event in man's history after his creation. While he was obedient he was ever with God, all that was God's on earth was his, and doubtless he would have been admitted to higher blessings, and a fuller participation hereafter. He disobeyed, and all was changed; driven out from his Father's presence, a barrier set up between him and God, he had lost all claim on every thing that was aforetime his. And in accordance with this the teaching of Holy Scripture is most plain, "As by one man's disobedience many were made sinners, so by the obedience of one shall many be made righteous ;" and in these words we are taught too to look to the true realization of the text. For it is of no one but of the God man, that the words can be in their fulness declared, " Son thou art ever with me, all that I have is thine."

Now by considering these two extremes we may learn a most practical lesson. In the first Adam we see disobedience and its results. In the second we see perfect obedience and its consequences. We know too well how many there are who have sinned, and yet do sin after the similitude of Adam's transgression. We have yet to learn how blessed may be our condition if we be conformed to the mind of Christ. Men do not realize sufficiently the gravity of the sin of disobedience. That, as it was the first, so is it in its essence the chief sin. And yet I venture to affirm that there is no one thing which our lord so emphatically declares to be of the greatest importance as obedience. "Not every one that saith unto me Lord, Lord, shall enter into the Kingdom of Heaven, but he that doeth the will of my Father which is in Heaven." "If ye love me keep my commandments." "He that hath my commandments and keepeth them, he it is that loveth me." "If a man love me he will keep my words." And listen to the sanctions. On these conditions, on none other mind, " he shall be loved of my Father, and I will love him, and manifest myself to him ;" which is explained, " My Father will love him, and we will come unto him, and make our abode with him." Do you see? Not only are we with God, according to the words of the text, if we be obedient, but God will be with us, and that not now and again, not fitfully, but for ever: " We will take up our abode with him." And in this promise we see not only the reward of obedience, but also the means whereby it is strengthened and sustained. If we be willing to keep God's commandments, if we do not even in heart wander from Him, He will fill us with the joy of His presence, and where He is no ill can come. It was because the heart was not tenanted that the evil spirit returned unto the once cleansed penitent, and the possession became sevenfold worse. There is an admirable illustration of this in one expression very often overlooked in the parable, which you so well know, of the unmerciful servant. We are sometimes amazed at his hardness after the mercy just shewn him. It is said "the same servant *went out* and found one of his fellow servants. It was a case of the common proverb, out of sight out of mind. But it surely meant to teach us that if we *go out* from the presence of God, we too shall fall into divers sins, which, while we remain consciously with Him, we shall be preserved from, because then He by His Spirit dwelleth in us and is with us.

It is only to men of such character that the highest best promises are made. When Christ says of His sheep that they shall never perish, and that no one shall pluck them out of His hand, the fulfilment of this gracious promise depends on the condition which is involved in the description of His sheep, viz. : "My sheep hear my voice, and I know them, and they follow me." No man, indeed, nor devil either, can hurt any who stay within the reach of God's protecting arm. But they can, alas how often they do, through their own wilfulness wander away themselves, and then they are no longer safe. I say not that they will be lost. This whole parable teaches us how diligently Christ seeks those who have wandered from the fold; how readily the Father forgives them on their return; but henceforth their happiness cannot but be chequered by self-reproach; their sense of security cannot but be marred by a recollection of how once they strayed; they have not the full blessedness nor peaceful rest of those who have ever kept within the fold, who have never striven to shake off the restraints, and so wander from the protection of the Everlasting Arms. And though their blessedness is great it lacks the fulness which they might, but for their own disobedience, have attained to.

It is hard, however, very hard, well nigh impossible,

for mortal man to realize the description, and therefore to appropriate the blessing of the text. It might be easier, first, if men would acknowledge the deep guilt of disobedience; secondly, if they would from the first prepare themselves to find it very difficult, if they would acknowledge that it entails in most cases suffering. The reason it is so difficult is because in most cases our will does not square with God's will; if we were perfect beings it might be otherwise; but as we are, there are so many lusts and passions, so many temptations from within and from without, which will lead us astray except we battle against them and resist them, that obedience cannot be other than difficult, cannot consist without self-denial, which comes naturally, as we say, to no man. Therefore it is that in so many cases, first in little things, by degrees in greater, we rebel against God's laws, and drift step by step into a condition of chronic disobedience, whence, as I have before remarked, the recovery is difficult and painful. Now, though the difficulty could never be less, our downward progress might be arrested, if we were diligent to examine our hearts and consciences, and if, recognizing the guilt of disobedience as such, we took ourselves to task for every rebellious thought unchecked, still more for every petty violation of law indulged. If our will were in conformity with God's will obedience would be easy. And we must strive to make it so, or else, hard as this may be, and vexatious as it may appear to us, it is nothing to the anguish and suffering which we shall have to bear, when, if by God's grace we be led to repentance, we contrast our sinful state with the perfect holiness of God, which ought to have been our model, not to mention the suffering of other kinds, whereby our Father, chastening us for our good, leads us to that repentance. We must boldly, yet with deep humility, face the fact declared by St. Paul concerning our blessed Lord that though He was a son, yet learned He obedience by the things which He suffered, and arm ourselves with the same mind. It is the only way of escaping the far greater, more enduring suffering which, when by God's grace we are penitent, the memory of our past sins must bring upon us. Forgiven they will be; blotted out, so as not to rise against us in judgment hereafter, in the blood of Christ; but undone they cannot be. They must run their course, and produce their consequences: and one of the most unfailing of these is the bitter recollections of them in time to come: a bitterness which will be all the greater the more perfect our repentance, the more spiritualized and subdued, and conformed to the law of Christ our affections. It is then simply a choice between the suffering which present self-denial entails, and that which follows, as the reward of disobedience and rebellion.

Do you not think that the eldest son in the parable had naturally the same desires, the same impatience of control, the same wish to be his own master as the younger one. There is no reason for doubting it. He however repressed them, and his brother indulged them, Hence the difference in their lives. And we have no reason to suppose that it was easier for him to act thus than for the prodigal; rather as the elder son the contrary would very likely be the case. It is a wonderful lesson, and one that demands that we ponder it well.

Try to realize the position of the two brothers the day, or the week, or the year, after the prodigal's return. I have said, we have no reason to suppose that the elder brother's jealousy endured longer than his father's answer. Conceive them then both living with their father—both doing his will—both receiving daily proofs of his love and tenderness. Doubtless both were supremely happy. But is there one here present who can doubt that often the younger son's heart must have been wrung by a sense of his own unworthiness, that every loving care of him, every affectionate word, every token of his Father's love, became not as St. Paul meant it, but as we too often mis-interpret it, " coals of fire heaped upon his head." How utterly undeserving he must have felt who had taken his share and wasted it, whenever he was treated not as he had in his humility asked, as a servant, but again as a son. But none of these cares, none of this anguish interrupted the peaceful rest wherewith the eldest son, who had never strayed, reposed on his father's love, and enjoyed as his own that which as the reward of his faithful service his father had made his.

Let us learn a lesson here, my brethren. While we thankfully, adoringly recognize the goodness and mercy of God, who will receive us even at the eleventh hour, if we truly repent, let us make it our constant aim to need no repentance, by living close to God, by setting Him alway before us, by never failing first to learn and then to do His will. We shall certainly fail, but the higher we set our aim the higher we shall reach. And we must remember the standard set before us is He of whom it was revealed in prophecy that He said, "Lo I come to do Thy will Oh God ;" who in the days of His flesh declared it to be His meat and drink to do God's will ; that He came down from Heaven not to do His own will but the will of Him that sent Him ; and who in the hour of His deepest agony thrice prayed, " Not my will but thine be done Oh Lord." We cannot, I repeat, attain to that perfection ; but we may strive after it ; we may resolve, God helping us, to put away all that rebels against God's will ; we may crucify our flesh with its affections and lusts ; we too may deny ourselves ; we may meditate deeply on the passion and cross of Christ, who suffered for our self-will and disobedience, whereby to inflame our hearts into a perfect surrender of themselves to Him. And all this we shall do, we must do, if we would even approximate to the highest blessedness, if we would be spared the bitter self-reproaches, which must otherwise, even after we be

forgiven, be our punishment. But if we do not, if we continue in our wanderings away from God,—I do not say we
run the risk of being cut off,—that though true, is beside
the question here,—I am desirous of bidding you emulate
the life and inherit the blessing of the elder son,—If, I say,
we continue to err and stray from God, we may be forgiven, but it will be at the cost of much suffering, which
we might have been spared, and though our blessedness
will be infinitely beyond our deserts, so unconceivably
great and good as to fill us with adoring love and grati-
tude, we shall still know and feel that we have missed
the highest place; which belongs to those who have never
wilfully sinned, and who shall hereafter be the brightest
saints in the Redeemer's Kingdom.